Everything You Need to Know About

GRIEVING

Grieving can cause strong feelings of sadness.

Everything You Need to Know About
GRIEVING

Karen B. Spies

Series Editor: Evan Stark, Ph.D.

THE ROSEN PUBLISHING GROUP, INC.
NEW YORK

Published in 1990 by The Rosen Publishing Group, Inc.
29 East 21st Street, New York City, New York 10010

First Edition
Copyright 1990 by The Rosen Publishing Group, Inc.

Manufactured in the United States of America.

Library of Congress Cataloging-in-Publication Data

Spies, Karen Bornemann.
    Everything you need to know about grieving/Karen Spies.
    (The Need to know library)
    Includes bibliographical references and index.
    ISBN 0-8239-1222-1
    1. Bereavement—Psychological aspects—Juvenile literature. 2. Loss
(Psychology)—Juvenile literature. I. Title. II. Series.
BF575.G7S65 1990
155.9'37—dc20   90-36541
                                           CIP
                                           AC

Contents

Introduction

Grief is the sadness we suffer when something special to us is gone. Usually we grieve over a death. But we also grieve over the loss of a pet or over a broken romance. Moving to a new home can cause grief. A divorce can also cause grief. You can probably think of many other causes, too. *? Can you think of some*

Sooner or later, everyone must grieve. When you grieve, you may have many different feelings. Grief makes everyone sad. Grief can sometimes cause anger. This kind of anger is often hard to understand. Grief also causes many questions. People often ask "Why did this have to happen?" "Why did it happen to *our* family?" *Have any of you felt this way?*

If you are grieving, you may wonder if anyone else has felt the anger or sadness you feel. You may feel so sad that you think your grief will never end.

Perhaps you have not yet suffered grief. No one close to you has died. You've never had to move. You may wonder how you will handle grief.

This book will help you learn to deal with losing someone or something important to you. It will help you understand your own feelings and fears about death. It will help you decide what to say and do when a friend or relative is grieving.

Grief can be so strong that people think their lives will never be normal again. It takes time to adjust to loss or change, but most people can handle it. Some people think grief will go away if you don't talk about it. But this is wrong. You need to talk about your feelings and fears. They will not go away unless you face them. They may hurt you for the rest of your life. By facing your fears and losses, and learning to live with your feelings, you will grow stronger.

If you are grieving, talk to someone who loves you. Talking may be hard at first. You may not wish to share all your feelings right away. But it is important to remember that you are not alone.

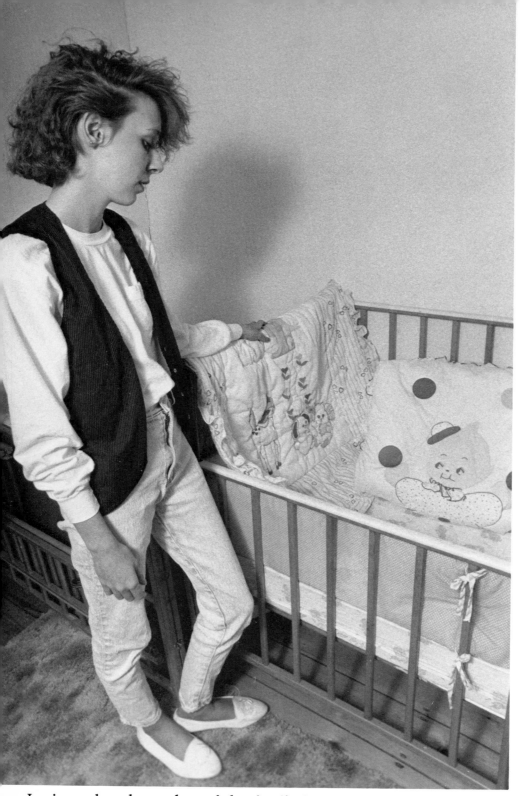

Losing a loved member of the family is a great shock.

Chapter 1

The Ways People Grieve

Grief is caused by loss or change. If a loved one dies, your life changes in many ways. When a romance ends, you feel lonely. If your family dog is hit by a car, you cry.

Each person grieves differently. Something that makes you sad may not bother your best friend. Let's look at what caused grief for three different kids.

"I cried all night, Sharon said. My dad told us he got a new job in another state. Now he won't have to be gone on so many business trips. But that means we have to move.

"I was born in this house. I've gone to school with the same kids for years. Now I have to go

to a new high school. My parents said I can help pick out our new house. I can even have a bedroom of my own.

"But I sure don't want to leave this neighborhood. How will I ever make new friends?"

Jim's one-year-old baby sister died. He said, "I didn't know what was going on for a few days. I knew Susie was sick, but I didn't know how sick. My parents were at the hospital all the time, but they never told me anything. I didn't know she was going to die.

"Then they left me at my aunt's house. They didn't let me go to the funeral. In fact, they didn't even tell me about it until it was over. They wanted to protect me. Like I was a little kid or something. That made me mad.

"My mom says she can't believe that Susie is dead. She cries all the time. She still won't let anyone else go into Susie's room. She wants to keep it exactly the way it was. My dad won't cry. He's started drinking a lot. He says he wishes this had happened to someone else.

"I wish my parents would just talk to me about Susie. But they don't talk to me about anything. They don't pay any attention to me anymore. It seems like they don't care about me at all. Don't they know that I'm still around?"

Tammy begins, "There was a boy in the band who liked my best friend. She danced with him a few times, and they saw each other at parties. Then he said he didn't want her to go out with anyone else. She just wasn't ready for that. He kept calling and calling. Finally, she told him she didn't want to hear from him again.

"The next week, he killed himself. I tried to tell my friend that it wasn't her fault. The boy had been taking drugs, and he wasn't doing well at school. He had just gotten kicked off the football team. He really had lots of problems.

"But my friend kept saying, 'If only I had been nicer to him. Then he wouldn't be dead.' I knew she was wrong, but I didn't know what to tell her."

The kids in these stories suffered grief in different ways. Sad things happened to them. They felt anger, guilt, or fear, which they did not want to face. But they had to.

People grieve in different ways. Grief can cause many feelings.

- **Shock**

An unexpected loss is shocking. You are numb. Shock made Jim's mom say "I can't believe my baby is dead."

- **Sadness**

Loss causes tears and sorrow. If you feel like crying, you should. Go in a room by yourself if you are embarrassed about crying. Boys need to cry, too.

- **Longing**

When you lose something that is important to you, you want it back. If your romance ends you think, "I don't want to be alone. How can I live without the one I love?" You know that wishing will not bring back what is lost. But you can't seem to help wishing that nothing had changed.

- **Anger**

Accidents and death often cause strong feelings of anger. People say, "Why did this happen? I did everything I was supposed to." They may blame the doctor or the hospital.

When a loved one dies, a person may feel anger. People ask, "If that person really loved me, why did he leave me?"

- **Fear**

Sharon was afraid. She did not want her family to move to a new town. She wondered, "What's going to happen to me?" Fear is a very normal part of grief.

- **Guilt**

Tammy's friend felt guilt. She wondered if the boy's death was her fault. Can you share some of the feelings you have felt

Sometimes people feel guilty about living when someone has died. It is not wrong to go on with your life. Even when you grieve, you will feel happy some of the time.

Shock, sadness, longing and all the other feelings are normal. They are part of mourning, the way we show our grief and sorrow. The length and kind of grief depend on the importance of the loss. Some people grieve more over the loss of a pet than the death of a person.

People used to wear black clothing for a year or more to mourn a loved one's death. Today there are no set rules about mourning. Some people wear black, others do not. Those who study grief say this is good. They know that no two people grieve alike.They also have learned that people need to grieve in order to get over their feelings of loss and their sadness. Different religions and cultures have different customs. But every culture and every religion has a way to deal with the feelings of grief, sadness, and loss caused by death.

Talking about grief helps you deal with your feelings. But it won't change what has happened. When you grieve, remember this Chinese proverb: "You can't keep birds of sorrow from flying over your head. But you can keep them from building nests in your hair." That means that you can feel grief without letting your feelings take over your life.

The loss of a pet is painful. Sometimes having the chance to say good-bye can make parting easier.

Chapter 2

What Causes Grief?

*J*eff's dog, Buster, always met him at the door
when Jeff came home from school. They played
catch with a ball. The dog never tired of the
game. Then Buster got sick. He stayed in his
dog bed most of the day. Jeff could tell it was
hard for Buster to move.

One day, when Jeff was at school, Buster died
in his sleep. Jeff's mom took Buster to the veteri-
narian (animal doctor). She didn't want Jeff to
see Buster's body.

Jeff cried when he found out that Buster was
dead. He was angry, too. He felt that he missed
the chance to say good-bye to his pet. Jeff was
surprised at his strong feelings.

Jeff's mom patted him on the shoulder. "Don't feel so bad, Jeff. I know you miss Buster, but we can get a new dog."

"I don't want a new dog," Jeff yelled. He ran to his bedroom and slammed the door.

Jeff is upset. His life has changed suddenly. Jeff misses his pet. He has powerful feelings, and he is not sure how to handle them.

Janelle and LaDonna were best friends. They both wanted to be cheerleaders. They practiced cheers together every day. Janelle did her best at the tryouts, but she was not chosen to be a cheerleader. LaDonna was.

"It's okay, Janelle. You'll make it next time," LaDonna said.

"No I won't. I'm never going to try out again. Being a cheerleader is so dumb." Janelle turned her back on LaDonna and wouldn't talk to her for days.

Then LaDonna asked Janelle to try out for the soccer team. She knew that Janelle could run fast and could kick the ball hard. But Janelle would not try out for the team.

Janelle is suffering. She is jealous of her friend. Janelle wanted to be a cheerleader very badly. Now she is afraid to try again. She is even afraid to try something else. She worries that she might not make the soccer team either.

Kim used to have lots of friends. She went steady with Yoshi. Her grades were good. Kim was happy with her life. Then her parents got a divorce. Her father moved out of the house. Her mother had to get a job. Kim had to do all the cleaning and cooking. She couldn't go out with Yoshi as often. When her friends had fun, Kim got angry. When they called on the phone, she wouldn't talk. After a while, they stopped calling.

Kim feels as if no one understands her problems. She misses her father. She is angry that she has so little time to spend with friends. She thinks no one has ever felt as bad as she feels now. She is sure she will never feel happy again.

Jeff, Janelle, and Kim are grieving. They wonder, "Why did this happen to me?"

That is a hard question to answer. Jeff did not do anything wrong. His pet was old and sick. It was time for Buster's life to be over. Janelle tried her best, but she couldn't force the judges to choose her as cheerleader. Kim could not stop her parents' divorce.

These kids feel very alone in their grief. You may feel this alone, too, if you are grieving. You may feel as if you have no control over your life. Try to remember that you cannot always keep bad things from happening. You cannot plan the times you will grieve.

Disbelief is often the first reaction when you hear about a death.

When you face grief, try not to blame anyone. What has happened is in the past. It is all right to feel sad. At the same time, you must decide to go on with your life.

It is important to face your feelings. Facing your feelings is called "grief work." It is not easy. But your grief feelings will not go away if you ignore them. How can you handle grief feelings? Let's look at what Jeff, Janelle, and Kim did.

Jeff wrote his mother a note about what was bothering him. She was glad Jeff had told her what was wrong. They cried together about Buster and hugged each other. They decided to get another pet later, when they both were ready.

Janelle went to see her school counselor. They talked about her feelings. Together they made a list of all the things Janelle enjoyed and did well. Janelle decided to help coach a girls' soccer team. The little girls on the team liked her very much. Working with the team made Janelle feel better about herself.

Kim asked her mom about the divorce. She found out there were many reasons for it. Both of her parents told Kim how much they loved her. They both found ways to spend more time with Kim. They hired a college student to help Kim with her school work. They gave Kim fewer chores, so she had more time to go out with Yoshi again. Kim called a friend, and soon other friends called her.

How do you handle grief feelings?

When you are grieving, try not to think about your problems all the time. Go out with your friends. Do your homework. Go to volley-ball practice. Doing these things will keep your grief out of your mind for a while. That will help you feel better.

If you still feel down, tell your mom or dad, or someone you trust. Talk to a good friend.

Some kids find it helps to write down their feelings. Some write poems, others draw pic-tures. You will need to find the way that works best for you. Do not keep your feelings to your-self. Remember, you are not alone.

It takes time to work out your grief.

Chapter 3

Learning To Talk About Death

*J*uan's grandmother had been ill for a long time. She was in the hospital. Then Juan's mother told him, "God took Grandma, because she was so good. God chose Grandma to be an angel."

Juan's mother wanted to protect him. She felt sad about Grandma's death. She was afraid to let Juan feel this sadness. Juan knew his grandmother was dead. He wished his mother would tell him the truth. He wondered why God let him live. He decided he must not be as good as his Grandma.

It is hard to face death. Sometimes it is even hard to say the word. But death will not go away if we ignore it. Death is a fact of life.

Someone is dying somewhere while you are reading this. Talking about death makes it seem less scary.

What is death? When a person is dead, breathing stops. Blood no longer flows through the body. When a person dies, all parts of the body stop working. The person cannot think or feel pain. The person cannot see or hear. Once people or animals die, they will always be dead.

Death used to be a part of everyday life. Most people died at home in their beds. Their family was with them when they died. Often, the kids were there, too. The family grieved over the death. But death was not so unexpected. It was a natural part of life. People who got sick often died. People could die at any time in their lives.

Little by little, death became less a part of daily life. Many diseases were cured. Now most people are old when they die. People usually die in a hospital. People do not want to talk about death, or even to think about it.

This is wrong. You need to talk about your feelings and fears. Otherwise they will not go away. They may be hurtful to you for the rest of your life. The most important part of sadness is learning to understand your feelings.

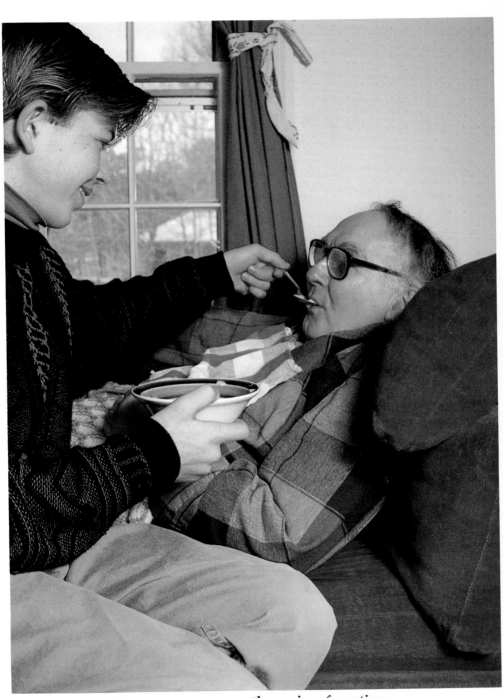

Caring for a dying person eases the pain of parting.

Sometimes people use other words for death. They say the dead person has "passed away," "is lost," or "has passed on." You need to say the word "dead." You cannot change death by using different words.

When Darin's father died, his aunt came over to the house. She put her arm around Darin. "Your dad is gone now. You must be brave, because you're the man of the house now."

Darin didn't feel brave. He felt alone. He wanted to cry, but he didn't think he should. That wouldn't be brave.

Darin's aunt loved him. She wanted to be helpful, so she said what she thought was right. But what she said was a mistake. It was not wrong for Darin to let his feelings out. He felt a terrible hurt, and he needed to cry.

There are many reasons why people and animals die. Most people die when they are old. Some people die of illnesses. Others die in accidents or wars. Sometimes people are murdered by other people.

Death is not a punishment, since everyone must die. Look outside and you will see plants that are dying. Look closely and you will see new plants coming up. The old that die make room for the new. It is the same with people

It is important to discuss your feelings with another person.

and animals. If people and animals never died, the world would run out of space and people would not have enough food to eat.

You may now have a pet, or you may plan to get one someday. You will love your pet, and take good care of it. You may feel as close to your pet as you do to a human friend. But pets, just like people, must die. When this happens, you will be sad and upset. You may feel many of the same feelings people have when a loved one dies. Sometimes the death of a pet can help you face your fears of death. That is a good thing.

Berta's grandfather died when she was ten years old. Her parents went to the funeral, but they made Berta stay home alone. Berta still remembers sitting in her room by herself. She loved her grandfather. She looked out the window and wondered what to do. She was crying, and she wanted someone to hug her.

Berta's grandfather was the only person she knew who had ever died. She missed him. And she was afraid. What if one of her parents died? What would she do?

Berta really needed to be comforted by her mom or dad. She needed them to remind her that they were both strong and healthy. She needed them to tell her she should not be afraid.

When someone you love dies, you need to express your feelings. Tell your mom or dad if you want to cry. Let them know you need hugs. Hug them, too. If you show your feelings, you may help your parents express theirs.

Part of facing death is knowing what to expect. People who are dying may look very different. They may lose a lot of weight, or they may be swollen. Sometimes a dying person's hair changes color or falls out.

When you visit, you may find it hard to talk to the person who is ill. You may feel uncomfortable, because you are not used to seeing the person the way he or she looks now. Remember that the person has not changed. He or she is the same person you have always known. Be ready to listen. Try to talk to the person the way you have in the past. Don't worry if the person seems sad.

If a loved one is dying at home, you will face many changes. Whoever is taking care of the person will have less time to spend with you. You may not be able to have friends over as often. Everyone will probably be more tired.

If this happens at your home, try to be understanding. Help to care for the patient (sick person). Stop in and talk to him or her about what you do during the day.

Sometimes a dying person goes to a hospice. A hospice is a nursing home for people who are dying. The people who work in a hospice can help your whole family. They are trained to help everyone face their fears of death.

If someone you know is dying, talking about your feelings will help you deal with what is happening. Ask your mom or dad any questions you have. Or talk to another adult you trust. A clergy member (a pastor, priest, or rabbi) is a good person to talk to about death.

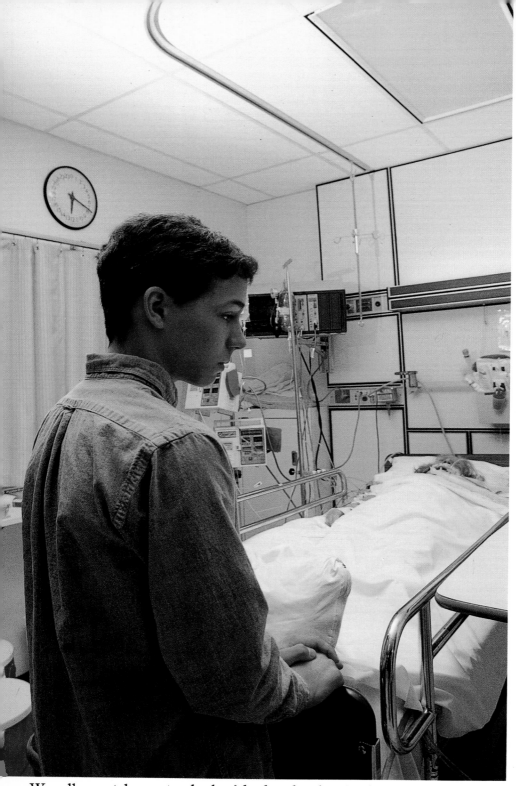

We all must learn to deal with the death of a loved one.

Chapter 4

Grandpa Died Today

Kayla was at a friend's house. Her mother called and said that Kayla's grandfather was dead. Kayla knew her grandfather had been sick. But she was surprised to hear that he died. Kayla felt guilty because she didn't feel very sad.

Marcus went to visit his grandmother in the hospital. She had cancer. She was very thin. Treatments had caused her to lose her hair. Grandma often fell asleep while Marcus was talking. He felt sad to see her like that. When Grandma died, Marcus felt relief. He knew she didn't feel pain anymore.

Maria spent the night at a friend's home. When her father picked her up, he said, "My sister died this morning."

At first Maria thought she heard him wrong. Then she felt like she should say something. But she didn't know what to say or what to do.

Kayla, Marcus, and Maria all have family members who died. Someday one of your relatives will die. This may already have happened to you. When someone you love dies, you will grieve. The more important this person was to you, the greater the pain you will feel when he or she dies.

You may have many different feelings after the death of a family member. If the person is older, the death may not surprise you. Marcus felt this way. His grandmother was old and very ill. He knew she would die soon.

You may feel guilty, like Kayla did. She was not upset when her grandfather died, because she did not know him very well. Kayla wanted to feel sadder, but she couldn't. If this happens to you, remember that everyone grieves in his or her own way. You may not feel great sorrow. This does not mean that you did not love the person who died.

The company of friends can help during the grieving process.

If someone dies after a long illness, you may be relieved. It is all right to feel relief. Marcus felt this way because he was glad his grandmother did not have to suffer any longer. Then he remembered how much he had loved his grandmother. He thought of how happy she was before she got sick. Marcus felt ashamed. He said to himself, "I shouldn't be happy that Grandma is dead." Marcus should not feel guilty. He is glad she is not in pain any longer. But he is sorry that she is dead.

When someone dies, you may feel shock. This can happen even when you expect the person to die. Maria was shocked to hear that her aunt had died. She did not know what to say or do. If you are not sure what to say, don't talk. Otherwise you may say something that is not helpful. Take the time to think about your feelings. Then speak when you are ready. Most people understand that facing death is hard for young people. They will know you care even if you can't express your feelings.

When you are grieving, other people may not know what to say to you. You may wish that they would go away and leave you alone. Such feelings are normal. Just remember that most people are trying to be helpful. They care about you. They want to do what they can to try to make you feel better.

Chapter 5

When A Parent Dies

Most kids worry at some time or other that one or both of their parents might die. Almost everyone has had this feeling. Luckily, most kids' parents do not die when the kids are young. But some do. If this happens to you, it is hard to believe. You may feel as if the world has come to an end. You may wish your life was over too. You will probably feel sorry for yourself. These are all normal feelings. Janna had many of them.

Janna's father was hit by a car when he crossed the street. At first she felt numb. How could this be happening to her? She thought bad things only happened to other people.

Janna began to worry a lot. She didn't feel like eating. She couldn't sleep very well at night because she often dreamed about her dad. She dreamed that he came to talk to her.

Then Janna was afraid. What if her mother died? What if something happened to her brother?

If your parent has just died, you may feel like Janna. You can't think much about the future. You feel as if you are living in a bad dream. If only you could wake up. Then the terrible sadness would go away.

People have these feelings even if they know ahead of time that someone is dying. Perhaps your parent had been sick for a long time. You might expect to be ready for the death. But even this kind of death is a shock. You cannot really prepare yourself for the death of someone you love.

People are the only living beings who know that they will die someday. Even though people know about death, it is still hard to understand. How could your parent die? How could this special person be dead?

This feeling is called disbelief. Disbelief is nature's way of helping you face death. It makes you feel numb. The numb feeling makes your pain a little less. It helps you face the fact of death.

If a parent dies, new responsibilities have to be accepted by other members of the family.

As time passes, you begin to miss the dead person very much. At first, you may be able to see your dead parent very clearly. You remember the smell of your mom's perfume, or your dad's shaving cream. You wish your mother or father could be there to hold you.

You may dream about your dead parent, like Janna did. Some kids find this a comfort. The dead person seems near to them again. In their dreams, they can feel happy.

As time goes by, your memories may fade in and out. Sometimes it will seem that the person is in the room with you. Other times you will not be able to remember the sound of the person's voice.

On some days, no matter how hard you try you will not be able to remember the dead person. This is scary. But it seems to be a normal part of grieving. Your mind and body are beginning to accept the death. Something inside of you is getting ready to let go of the parent.

Once you can let go, and accept the death, your memories come back. Now they seem to be memories about good feelings and happy times together. You will remember things like your mom's favorite joke, or the way your dad sang in the shower.

Little by little, you begin to understand that your parent is never coming back. This usually happens many months after the person has died. You may cry harder at this time than when you first found out about the death. That's okay.

Then you may feel scared. You wonder what will happen to you. Who will take care of you from now on? Along with these worries you may feel jealousy, anger, or guilt. Shawn, Kelly, and Greg had these feelings.

Shawn's father died when Shawn was fifteen. Shawn said, "My dad died just when I was getting to know him. He didn't get to see my first touchdown. I know he would have been proud of me. I felt like his death cut off a whole beginning. I never got a chance to know him as an adult."

Shawn felt cheated. When he saw other boys with their fathers, he was jealous. These are normal feelings.

Kelly wanted to go to a dance at school. All her best friends were going. Her mother wouldn't let her. Kelly was so angry that she said, "You never let me do anything. All I ever do is work. I wish you were dead!"

A couple of months later, Kelly's mother died in a skiing accident. Kelly had wished for her mother to die. Now her mother was dead.

It was not Kelly's fault that her mother died. She did not die because Kelly was angry at her. There is nothing Kelly could have done to make things different.

Kelly knew her mother's death was not her fault. But she still felt guilty about her angry words.

Greg's dad died of a heart attack. Greg's mom had to go back to work. Sometimes she said things like "Why did your dad leave me like this? I just can't make it alone." Greg was scared when his mom talked that way.

Greg's mom did not mean what she said. She was angry because she felt such great pain. As time went on, Greg worried less. His mom loved him, and she wouldn't leave him.

Janna, Shawn, Kelly, and Greg had many normal feelings of grief. They felt sadness, shock, anger, worry, guilt, and fear. Facing these feelings and dealing with them is part of grieving. With time, you will be able to let these feelings go.

Another part of grieving is adjusting to changes. You will face many changes when a parent dies. You may have to live in a new place. You may have to help out more at home. If your father has died, your mother may have to work full-time to earn money to support the family. If you are old enough, you might want to get a part-time job.

Give yourself time to face these changes. You will feel sadness for a long time. But after many months, you will probably feel less pain.

Be patient during the time that your family is trying to decide what to do next. Try to make the best of each day. Share with others the things that bother you. Together you can face this difficult time.

When you lose a loved one, keeping good memories alive helps.

Expressing your feelings is important in accepting a death.

Chapter 6

She Was Too Young To Die

*T*eena's sister Carrie died from taking drugs. *Teena said, "How can I go out with my friends and laugh and have fun? I hurt too much. I can't believe that Carrie is gone. I feel so angry. She was so young."*

Bruce's girlfriend Nancy had a blood disease. She died when she was sixteen. Bruce said, "I never thought about dying until Nancy died. I won't ever see her cute freckled face again. She won't ever beat me at checkers again. And it happened so fast. One day she was laughing and alive. The next day she was dead. Who knows. Maybe I'll be the next one to go."

Peter's baby brother died. "We never got to take Bobby home from the hospital. It seems so unfair. Bobby never got a chance to do anything."

One of these stories may sound like what has happened to you. Or your story might be different. But these kids and many others have grieved over the death of a child or a teenager.

When a young person dies, you may feel angry. You may feel that he or she did not have a chance to enjoy life. Both Teena and Peter were angry. Anger is a hard feeling to face. But you must try to talk about it. You cannot get over your grief if you feel anger.

You may also worry, like Bruce did, that you are going to die soon. But the death of someone your age will not cause you to die.

Twelve-year-old Laura cannot imagine what this Christmas will be like without her four-year-old sister, Tina. Tina died of a brain tumor. The whole family had delighted in Tina's joy at Christmas.

Kevin's best friend Joey died of cancer. They had gone to camp together every summer. They had walked to school together every day for seven years. Kevin will be starting Junior High in September. He doesn't know how he will be able to walk to school that first day, and every day, without his friend.

Perhaps the most difficult loss you will have to bear as a young person is the death of a sibling or a friend. Most people live long and healthy lives. But sometimes death comes to someone young. This kind of death may seem even greater than the death of an adult. We grieve for the things a young person didn't get to do, or to be. We grieve because we will miss a friend or sibling we expected to grow up with. We realize how many things they will never be able to share with us. We will miss them at family celebrations, and very special occasions.

Your grief may make it hard to keep up in school. You may find that you forget things easily. The other kids may seem happy and busy. This might make you angry. All this is a normal part of grieving. Be patient. After a while you won't feel quite so down. You will be able to keep your mind on other things.

Even after you get over feeling anger, pain, and loss every time you think about your sibling or friend, it will take a long time to heal. Remembering things you shared will hurt a lot in the beginning. Your pain may last a long time. You will always have memories. But after time has passed, the pain will lessen.

Some kids find that talking with friends is helpful. Others like to write down their thoughts. Drawing pictures about feelings may also help to ease your pain.

Death is never easy to understand. The death of a young person is especially hard. No one knows why some people live and others die.

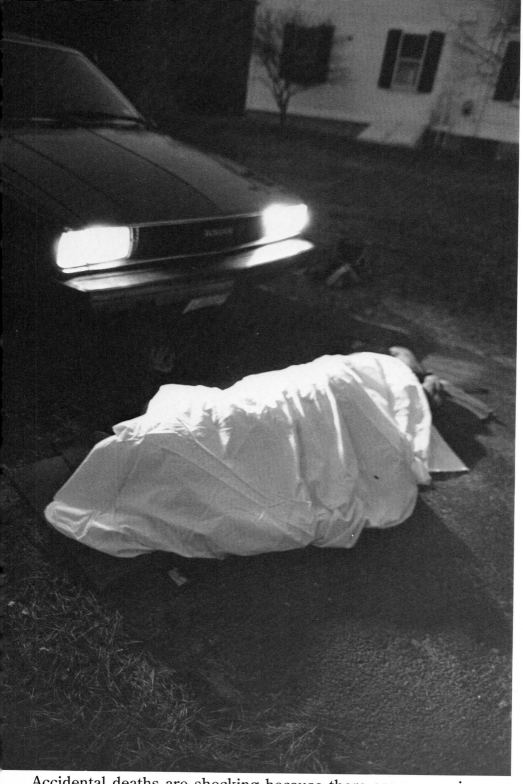

Accidental deaths are shocking because there are no warnings.

Chapter 7

I Didn't Get To Say Good-Bye

*S*eth's *sister died in a boating accident. Seth and his family were shocked and numb. Joy was only seventeen. She had looked forward to the boat trip for many months. Now she was dead.*

Seth dreamed that he could have saved Joy. He was supposed to go on the trip, too, but he had gotten sick. "If only I had been there," Seth thought. "I am a great swimmer. I could have helped Joy."

Accidental Deaths

Joy died by accident. Accidental deaths are very shocking, because they happen without notice. You have no way to prepare for such a death. There is usually very little you could do to keep such a death from happening.

Sudden deaths often cause many guilt feelings. Seth wondered, "Could I have helped my sister? Did she suffer?

A good way to face guilt is to say out loud, "I feel guilty. I wish I had done something different." As soon as you name what you are feeling, it will be easier for you to face it.

You may feel like screaming, or crying loudly, when you think about this kind of a death. It is normal to have these feelings. Be sure to tell a parent or another adult what is bothering you. Then they will not worry about you when you show such strong feelings.

Remember that each person has his or her own way to grieve. Playing a hard game of tennis may make you feel better. Talking with a good friend may help. Find what works for you. Doing things that make you feel better will help you to deal with your fears. You will grow stronger inside. Then it will be easier for you to face death.

Kareem was eighteen. He had finished high school, but he was still living with his parents. Each time Kareem started a new job, he quit after a few months. He wasn't able to make many friends.

Kareem had tried to commit suicide (kill himself) two times. He had already planned his funeral service.

Kareem's mother thought he would feel better if he lived in his own place. Kareem pretended to be happy about moving, but inside he was afraid.

His parents helped him move. That very night, Kareem took sleeping pills and died. His mother blamed herself for Kareem's death.

Suicide

When someone commits suicide, the person's family and friends may feel the death is their fault. Kareem's mother knew death was what he wanted. But she still felt there must have been some way she could have stopped Kareem.

At least 6,000 teenagers like Kareem kill themselves each year. As many as one million try to commit suicide.

Why do these kids want to die? People who commit suicide feel as if no one understands them. They feel lonely or unloved. They often say, "No one cares if I live or die," or "You would be doing so much better without me." Some of these young people complain of family problems. Others blame their poor jobs or their use of drugs. To those who commit suicide, death seems like a way to get rid of the pain they feel. People who kill themselves do not think about how much their death will hurt their friends and family.

Kids who think about killing themselves often show signs of how they feel. They are depressed (they feel very down, very sad). They may talk about wanting to die. They may give away their favorite things. This is part of their way of getting ready to die. Often, they refuse to talk to family members about their feelings.

If anyone you know talks or acts this way, get help. Tell your parents or another adult you trust. Look in the back of this book for places to call for help.

If you ever feel so depressed that you think you want to die, tell someone right away. Don't let the hopeless feelings grow.

Other Sudden Deaths

Sometimes young people die in violent ways. They are killed by another person, or they die in a war. These kinds of deaths do not happen often. They may be the hardest kinds of deaths to face, because they seem so unfair.

No one likes to talk about sudden death. Accidents, suicide, wars, and murder are hard to think about. They seem to be such a waste of life. But these kinds of death must be faced, too. The most important thing to remember is this: You are not alone, no matter how bad life may seem. You can find comfort. After a time of grieving your life will start to feel normal again.

Chapter 8

After A Loved One Dies

*W*hen Steve was fourteen and Tara was eight, their uncle died. Steve's parents talked to their pastor about the funeral. "Steve and Tara loved their uncle so much. They are too young to go to the funeral, aren't they? They may become upset if they see their uncle's body."

The pastor said, "Ask Steve and Tara what they want to do. The funeral is an important time. It gives everyone a chance to share in the service for the dead person. It's a good way to honor the life of the person who died."

Steve and Tara's parents wanted to protect them from death. But this is not good. Funerals and memorial services are a special part of mourning. They help the friends and family of the dead person to grieve together. They offer a time to share religious beliefs. They are a

way for the living to say good-bye to the one
who has died.

Before the funeral, the body of the dead
person is usually taken to a funeral home. That
is a special place where people can go to visit
with the dead person's family. The body is
dressed and laid out in a casket. The casket
(also called a "coffin") is the box or chest used
to bury the body. Most often the casket is kept
in a special room at a funeral home. Visiting
hours are set. People who knew the dead person can come to comfort the living members of
the family. Sometimes the casket is open, so
people can view the body. It is helpful to some
people who are grieving to be able to see the
dead person one more time.

You may worry about looking at the body.
Remember that the body is still part of the person you loved. But do not feel ashamed if you
decide not to view the body. Many people pre-
fer to remember someone they love from life.

Different cultures have different funeral customs. Some people have times *before* a funeral
for friends and family to get together. A *wake*
is a time when people get together to remember
fondly someone who has died. Sometimes
people visit in special rooms in funeral homes.
Family members take comfort from other
people's good memories of someone they love.

Neighbors and friends can comfort grieving families.

People visit grieving Jewish families *after* a
funeral. Many Jewish families observe a mourning period (*shiva*) that lasts for several days.
During that time family members express their
sadness, and friends come to comfort them.
After the *shiva* is over, the family is supposed to
try to behave normally again.

The funeral may be held at a church or syna-
gogue, or at the funeral home. A clergy member (pastor, priest or rabbi) will read from the
Bible and pray. He or she will talk about special times in the life of the dead person. Sometimes friends or family members will read
poems or say prayers. One or more songs may
be sung.

The funeral is a time for family and friends to
comfort each other. People will cry. It is all
right to cry at a funeral. Crying is one way to
show how much the dead person will be
missed.

The dead person may be buried at a ceme-
tery. Sometimes the body is cremated. Crema-
tion changes the body to ashes by burning.
The ashes are clean and white. They may be
stored in a small jar or urn. Sometimes the
ashes are buried.

Some people decide to donate certain parts
of their bodies to medicine. They sign a special
letter so people know this is what they want to
be done. Doctors can then transplant the body

parts, such as corneas (parts of the eyes), the heart, kidneys or other organs. These are used to help living people. The body part is taken only after the person has died.

There are many ways to show sympathy to the dead person's family. Some people send cards, special notes, or flowers. Others choose to donate money in memory of the dead person. The money is sent to a group that the dead person supported, such as the American Cancer Society, or the March of Dimes.

The family of the dead person also needs everyday help at first. They are probably still in shock. Many people bring food. They offer to help with tasks such as cleaning or shopping.

Another important way to help is by listening and talking to a person who is grieving. Both visits and telephone calls are helpful. Perhaps you know someone who is mourning. Think about what you would like if you were grieving. This will help you know what to do and say.

When you are grieving, don't be afraid to share your feelings. Someone will ask, "How are you?" You may answer, "I'm fine." This is how you want to feel. This is probably what the other person wants to hear. But deep inside, you may not feel fine. Then you should say something such as, "I really feel down today. I need to be with someone. Could you come over for a while?"

Getting back into social activities helps the recovery process.

Chapter 9

Recovering From Grief

Grieving is something each of us must do all by ourselves. You will grieve in your very own way. Your grief cannot be hurried. Doctors say that grief over the death of a loved one can last as much as two years. Recovering from other kinds of grief may not take as long. The hurt never truly goes away. Slowly, you learn to live with your feelings. After a while, they are easier to bear.

As your life returns to normal, you may face more changes. That is what happened to Ronnie and Justine.

Ronnie is sixteen. He used to live in a big house with his mom, dad, and two sisters. Ronnie stayed after school some days for swim team practice. His mom worked part-time, but she was always there when he came home from school.

Six months ago Ronnie's parents got a divorce. His dad moved to an apartment. "At first we had enough money," Ronnie said. "But now Mom has to go to work full-time. That means I'll have to take care of my sisters after school. I have to quit the swim team. I thought I handled the divorce well. I didn't like it, but I figured I didn't have much choice. But now I have to face all these other changes."

Justine's dad died last year. Recently, her mom has started to go out on dates. Lately, she has brought Max home quite a few times. Max is divorced. He has two girls of his own. Justine wonders what will happen if her mom and Max get married. Will she have to move? What if she has to share a room with one of Max's girls?

"I was just getting used to Dad being gone," Justine said. "My life was beginning to settle down. Now it looks like it's going to be messed up again."

It is never easy to face change. Life is not "fair." Somehow you must find a way to live within an unfair world. Remember that all families face change, not just grieving families.

You may keep asking, "Why did this happen to me? I don't feel like I'm getting any better." But you need to try to face each day—one day at a time.

Sometimes the grief feelings get so strong that you don't think you can handle them. Or perhaps they go on so long that normal activities don't seem important anymore. That's what happened to Brian.

Brian's father has been dead for a year. Brian has about twenty pictures of his dad along one wall in his room. He has his dad's hockey skates hung by the closet. His dad's pen set sits on Brian's desk. He begs his mom to take him to watch the hockey team his dad played on. After dinner each night, Brian listens to tapes of the family talking and joking. He loves to hear his father's voice. Brian doesn't call his friends anymore.

Brian is spending all his time remembering his dad. When he was alive, Brian's father didn't do much with him. Now Brian is dreaming about the life he wishes he'd had with his father. The way Brian is acting is not helping him get over his grief.

It is normal for Brian to be sad. But Brian's feelings have gone on for too long a time. His feelings have changed everything that he does.

Some teens may need help from a counselor or therapist to adjust after a death in the family.

What should you do if something like this happens to you? Talk to a friend or parent. There are also many other people who can help. Try talking to your doctor, or your pastor, priest, or rabbi. Your school counselor might suggest a support group. People in a support group all have problems that are alike. They meet to give each other help and support.

In the back of this book there is a list of places to call for help. Do not be afraid to seek help. Everyone goes through troubled times. If you broke your arm, you wouldn't try to fix it yourself. When you feel pain inside, you need someone who is trained to help people to deal with such problems.

Every time you grieve, you learn. Certain things in life cannot be changed. You can let them bother you. Or you can decide to start making your life work well just the way it is. That is what Marcy, Sam, and Fran did.

Marcy had gone with Ahmad for two years. They broke up before the prom. Missing the prom made Marcy very sad. The next day, Marcy found out she had won a basketball scholarship. Now she could afford to go to college. Ahmad had taught her to shoot baskets. She will always be glad that they knew each other.

Sam's dad taught him how to draw. They enjoyed going on hikes together and drawing pictures of the birds and animals they saw. When Sam was twelve, his dad died. Now Sam is grown up. He is a famous artist. His animal pictures are in many books. Sam says, "Every time I draw a picture, I thank Dad for what he taught me."

Fran is fourteen. She has heart disease. No one knows how much longer Fran will live. Right now she goes to school and she feels good. But this could change at any time. Fran knows she is dying. "But so is everyone else. They just don't know it. I try not to waste any time being sad. It's not easy, but it's what I have to do."

The more you think about grief and sadness, the more you will be thankful for happy times. You cannot hide from grief. It is a part of life. By facing it, you will learn a lot about yourself. By facing it, you will keep the birds of sorrow from building nests in your hair.

Glossary—*Explaining New Words*

casket A wooden box in which a body is buried. Also called a coffin.

clergymember A pastor, priest, or rabbi.

cremate To change a body to ashes by burning. The ashes can be kept in a small jar or urn.

depressed Very sad. If you are a little depressed, you might say you are "down."

funeral A memorial ceremony before the burial of someone who has died.

hospice A place where dying people go to receive care.

memorial service A service in memory of someone who has died. An event where people can remember a loved one, and comfort one another.

mourning The way we show grief or sorrow. Some people wear black clothing when they mourn a loved one's death.

suicide The act of taking your own life (killing yourself) on purpose.

support group People who have problems that are alike. They get together to help each other.

Where To Get Help

If you feel as if you want to die, or you think one of your parents may commit suicide, there is another way to get help. Call 1-800-555-1212. Ask the operator for the telephone number of SUICIDE HOTLINE. The operator will tell you another number to call which begins 1-800. There is no charge for calling "800" numbers.

The Compassionate Friends can help if your brother or sister has died. To find the support group nearest you, contact:

Compassionate Friends
P.O. Box 1347
Oakbrook, Illinois 60521
312-323-5010

Sometimes, when a parent dies, kids need to be with an adult of their same sex. Big Brothers of America helps a boy find a man to spend time with; Big Sisters is for girls.

Big Brothers or Big Sisters of America
220 Suburban Station Building
Philadelphia, Pennsylvania 19106

Make Today Count is for people dying of cancer. Get the address of the group nearest you from:

National Make Today Count Office
P.O. Box 303
Burlington, Iowa 52601
319-753-6521

For Further Reading

Blume, Judy. *Tiger Eyes*. Scarsdale, NY: Bradbury Press, 1981. (Fiction) In this story, Davey Wexler and her brother and mother learn to deal with the murder of Davey's father.

Hyde, Margaret O. and Lawrence E. Hyde. *Meeting Death*. New York: Walker and Company, 1989. The authors cover many ways to deal with feelings about death, including suicide.

Schleifer, Jay. *Everything You Need To Know About Teen Suicide*. New York: The Rosen Publishing Group, Inc., 1989. This book is a guide to the causes of teen suicide. It deals with the danger signals to look for in yourself and others.

LeShan, Eda. *Learning To Say Good-by: When A Parent Dies*. New York: Avon Books, 1988. The author uses examples from real families to talk about how to handle the death of a parent.

Rofes, Eric E. and The Unit at Fayerweather Street School. *The Kids' Book About Death and Dying*. Boston: Little Brown and Company, 1985. This book was written by fourteen students, ages 11 to 14, and their teacher. They talk about how and why death happens and give ideas about what to do when someone you love dies.

Index

About the Author
Karen Bornemann Spies was an elementary school teacher and vice
principal before embarking on a second career in publishing. She
has written school curriculum as well as several books for young
people. Currently, Ms. Spies teaches writing at the community
college level and offers workshops for young writers. She lives
with her husband and two children in Colorado, where she teaches
skiing on the weekends.

About the Editor
Evan Stark is a well-known sociologist, educator, and therapist as
well as a popular lecturer of women's and children's health issues.
Dr. Stark was the Henry Rutgers Fellow at Rutgers University, an
associate at the Institution for Social and Policy Studies at Yale University, and a Fulbright Fellow at the University of Essex. He is the
author of many publications in the field of family relations and is
the father of four children.

Acknowlegdments and Photo Credits

Photographs by Barbara Kirk

Design/Production: Blackbirch Graphics, Inc.
Cover Photograph: Blackbirch Graphics, Inc.